EDIBLE GRACE

Lyrical Micro-Prose by

GUY BIEDERMAN

Edible Grace
Lyrical Micro-Prose
By Guy Biederman

ISBN: 978-0-9980375-4-7

Publication date: September 2019

Published by KYSO Flash Press: http://www.kysoflash.com
Bellingham, Washington, USA. Printed in the USA.

Please send questions and comments to the Publisher:
KYSOWebmaster@gmail.com

Or, contact the Author via his website:
https://www.guybiederman.com/

Dedicated to Penny

Also by Guy Biederman

Soundings and Fathoms
(Finishing Line Press, 2018)

House Samurai
(Iota Press, 2006)

Parts & Labor
(Thumbprint Press, 1992)

Table of Contents

The life so short, the craft so long to learn.

—the first line of *Parlement of Foules*, by
Geoffrey Chaucer (c. 1343–1400)

The Moose & the Fly

A moose can feel a fly land on its antlers. So why can't I feel when you leave the bed? There is resistance in the air, conflict between molecules who wish to occupy the same space. What about molecules who don't wish to occupy the same space? The moose who wants no fly on its antler; the fly who wants no part of the moose. Maybe the moose calls the fly a parasite, annoying. The fly accuses the moose of moose-splaining. Is it possible to look the other way, find a new place to land for a while, thinks the fly. Is it possible to ignore this fly on my antlers, thinks the moose; or just accept its light presence on part of me that I can't see? Where's the harm? That field of grass looks sweet and green, the flowing stream, inviting. I'll go with this flow. And so will I, thinks the fly, tasting sap on the antler's tip through its feet in its brief world of silence before the moose enters the stream and the fly jumps backwards and flies off on its way.

Rue de la Bûcherie

Walking down a street in Paris with your ex, she with pace, you more of a stroll, you reach for her hand and she reaches for yours. And it's not anything. Not anything like that. Like holding hands might seem to an outside observer. It's a connection not leading to a kiss or lovemaking. It's just a way you both say hi, how are you, I remember you, I remember our dreams, our kisses, our feelings and here we are in Paris walking together, but yeah at different speeds, different strides, and then you both let go and she disappears into the crowd and you glance at your reflection in the window of a bookshop and wander in to find the books of your friends on the shelf, and yours— poems inspired by the one whose hand you no longer hold.

Bathrobe, Biscotti, & Bike

Truman watched from the kitchen window as Fiona walked to the bus stop carrying her billboard briefcase which included the lunch he'd made for her.

He hummed along with Mozart as he rinsed the breadboard, did a little tai chi as he put away the bread, the jelly, and the extra chunky peanut butter.

Something caught his eye.

He bent down to the checkered linoleum and peered closely. It was the chocolate-dipped biscotti, individually wrapped, that he'd tucked into her bag as a surprise. It must've fallen out when she re-packed her billboard briefcase.

He picked it up and brought it close to his nose. Such a perfect treat. "Your safety," he said, feeling ravenous, "cannot be guaranteed."

Truman ran outside, forgetting he was still in his robe, but instantly aware he was barefoot by the cold slab of concrete. Fiona's bus pulled away. He hopped on the bike of his 8-year-old neighbor Sam and began pedaling. The bus had one more stop before the freeway. With a bit of good fortune—perhaps a commuter with inexact change—he just might catch it.

For he was no ordinary stay-at-home retired house-spouse in a robe, Kleenex in his pockets—he was Bathrobe Man with a job to do. Gripping the individually wrapped biscotti firmly between his teeth, Truman held on to the handlebars with both hands and pedaled hard, bathrobe belt blowing in the wind behind him.

Animal Ally

I'm in breathing class, trying to hold my own, and the instructor wants us to call up our animal ally. This is always the hardest part and I desperately want to come up with something, anything, like everyone else. My breathing gets faster. I start to panic. I think of a cat, only I'm allergic to cats, and I start to sneeze and my eyes get red so I quick change it to a dog—but I've been afraid of dogs since I was six when the neighbor's Jack Russell took a chunk out of me, so I'm breathing hard, sweating like a pig and the instructor sees I'm not breathing right while everyone else in the class is doing so perfectly, and she starts to walk over, and I think—crap, I have no animal allies in this world—not one. I can't even breathe right. I am such a loser.

Then I remember, my savior, my ally, my very own higher self. My eyes go to the corner of the room, to the ancient, intricate cobweb covering the dirty window. I lock onto the spider with my spirit gaze, feel my breath begin to slow, look around, smiling, smiling into my breath just like the teacher says. But, oh no, the guy next to me in blue spandex is looking at the same corner, that copy cat, and I say, Oh no you don't buster, she's mine, get your own dang animal ally. I start to breathe hard, chug even, it's a race to the finish line, and at the last second I hook him with my elbow, well more a nudge really, and he falls back on his mat and I smile, smile into my breath, which is perfect now, triumphant and grim.

How Do We Get Back Into the Zoo?

You don't know how you get into these sorts of things, and for years you didn't know how to get out of them. But here you are once again, this time at a party thrown by Giraffes, and you're feeling not only short, but hungry, too. You hate leaf appetizers and the smell of eucalyptus makes you woozy. Now you're trapped in the corner with a sad-faced ape who, by his reckoning and with tacit agreement from his girlfriend, Toucan Pam, is a card-carrying genius. Carnivores are all afraid of being laughed at, he says. Herbivores are afraid of being killed. Know what I mean, know what I mean? He punches your shoulder for emphasis. You try to ignore, but find yourself knocked a little off balance. Sad Face doesn't notice. Toucan Pam does. She smiles as a cracker disappears inside her extraordinary beak. You try not to stare. Sad Face won't stop. The world's a colossal mess, he goes; Giraffes are nice enough, but they walk around with their heads in the clouds. Am I right, am I right?

He revels in his cleverness, revealing huge yellow teeth, red gums. This time you dip your shoulder before his playful punch connects, and resist the urge to sink your pearly whites into his long hairy arm. Not so playfully. You look around for Kailey, that cute coyote you were hoping would show, it being close to sundown. Spotted skunk holds court near punch-bowl pond. Industrious gophers make mounds on the shore near a bumper crop of cattail reeds. A frog bellows. Another answers. You're thinking, *I'm outta here*. But Sad Face has cut off your exit and now a hippo joins in. They stare at you. You wolves don't talk much do you, says Sad, cat got your tongue?

Toucan Pam cracks up and her bird friends join in a cacophony of bird sputter and laughter, and you think, *gadzooks, does everyone know how badly it ended between me and Lady Panther?* It hadn't exactly been a fair fight when her oafish bear friend sat on your tail and pinned you to the tundra as you were finishing your rabbit stew.

You growl back at Sad Face—wolves don't bark. It's so beside the point, but you don't care to explain. Pam gets it. Sad Face shakes his sorry head and scratches himself. You evaluate your options: go for his throat or exit stage left…when at that moment, Leo the lion and his pride make an entrance.

The soiree grows quiet. Giraffes stop chewing. Everyone freezes as Leo and company saunter with impressive ease, and you're thinking, *well, now it's a party*. You slip into the shadows of tall trees, pleased to get away from the boorish ape without bloodshed. A rabbit twitches an ear. Someone squeaks, Anyone know how we get back in the zoo? The ape can't help himself, raises both arms and screeches, Buy a ticket, dummy! Leo and his pride are on him in an instant and they devour old Sad Face, genius card and all, while everyone watches from a respectful distance. Behind you Kailey quietly whispers, Wanna bounce? And off you go.

Mr. Shortcut

I call my boyfriend apostrophe because he's so possessive. He calls me enigma because I'm not.

I'm married, I say. Hire a double he says, to go through the motions of your life.

But emotions are my bread and butter. Why hire a Sherpa to pack your gear up the hill? Dad was Mr. Shortcut. Always after a quicker route to Uncle Stout's, though he hated iced tea and saying grace before a Sunday lunch of oniony enchiladas—beneath an abstract watercolor of the holy trinity painted by cousin Vince one summer in jail.

Be with me, pleads apostrophe. Stay away, I say—only luring him closer. We're a pair of docks on a shameless sea. A misplaced metaphor, an ill-conceived pun, a comma coupling two thoughts, trying to be one.

Paper Clip Mechanics

You take a paper clip—with its simple, functional design, its etch-a-sketch lines—and twist it into a two-legged creature with no head or arms. You straighten it out and turn it into a pipe cleaner covered in resin. Into a scratch awl and carve initials into your locker, next to the scrawlings made by others before you, a paper-clip registry of sorts. You discover its utility as a key to open locks, and handcuffs. You shape it into a circle whose ends don't quite meet up, and realize, once bent, it can never be bent back to its original shape, to hold, say, this sheath of papers you would like to organize and keep together—these stories of your life. You look at your crooked fingers, your crooked handwriting, your slant on the world, and now your crooked paper clip, with its principles of torsion and history of resistance. You decide that this sheath of papers will make do as a loose pile that will get shuffled, lost, recycled, or some day trashed and you understand it's not the keeping of them together, the organizing of them for eternity, or the semester, or the rest of the calendar year that matters, but the moments spent uncovering simple epiphanies, like the wonder of the paper clip and its simple design, the flowing of ink on the page, the momentary meaning of this life, and the unfolding of function into new shapes yet unborn, yet unbent.

When You're Hungry Enough

Grasshoppers and crickets chirp for a reason: to call a nearby mate, to celebrate having mated, to warn away a rival. That's animal fact. That's purpose.

A group of grasshoppers is called a cloud; a group of crickets, an orchestra. A group of canaries is a charm. Canaries were the first caged songbirds. The Spanish thought of that.

First cricket in a jar, captured by a kid who punched holes in the lid so the cricket could breathe. So they could hear the cricket sing. So they could watch the cricket die. Maybe not their intent. That's Unexpected Consequences 101.

That's what happens when we put things in jars, in boxes, in cages. Their songs become the songs of those not captured, those who live in a charm, in a cloud, in a roar of free verse, who sing of those encaged so no one forgets,

who sing about the depravity of captivity, the cruel disregard
of concrete, because it has come to that, the best poems come
when we have something

to say and have to say it, when we find the chair, punch the keys,
carve the pen,

because we are calling, we are hungry, we are ravenous.
We are warning.

Breakfast at the Low Tide Café

iPad Island

"I remember going to the tire store with my dad as a kid," says Steve. "He always bought retreads, though I didn't know what retreads were at the time. I just loved going with him—loved the smell of new tires, fresh rubber."

Marie nods, staring at her iPad. But Steve doesn't know if she's nodding at his story, or the Words With Friends game she's got going with Mary. One of them. She's got dozens going at a time—he wonders if there's a 12-step for it.

Steve looks around the lobby of Les Schwab Tires, glances at the soundless TV playing a cooking show.

"Think we should get the wheels aligned too? It's extra you know."

Marie nods again.

He considers.

"Think I should go to Tahiti with our marriage counselor, Terry?"

Marie nods.

Aha. "And should we never come back again?"

She nods again, still staring at her screen. He sees a green glow on her red face and thinks, *is that weird or what?* What is the new weird? He hears the whirring of pneumatic wrenches in the garage removing lug nuts in quick bursts, imagines the wheels coming off.

"So if you were on a desert isle and you could only bring one thing with you, what would you choose—me or Words With Friends?"

He glances off towards an aisle of Michelins. Feels a tingle—no—a vibration. Checks his phone.

A text.

From her: YOU, silly—there'd be no wifi on the island :)

Pillow Fight

Haley swings the pillow and connects, and spit flies from the side of Sam's mouth and the fight is on. She's got surprise on her side and a couple of inches on him, too, but the force of contact surprises even her, and she remembers now how firm the $80 custom pillow is.

Sam looks stunned for a moment, and in that split second it could go either way. But he's swayed by Haley's revealing nightie as she heaves, slightly catching her breath, and let's face it, admiring her shot. He grabs the soft pillows she sleeps on and goes to work (the memory foam in his left, and feather in his right), pummeling the sides of her head. Haley's laughing and covering up, moving closer, and though Sam's connecting, the soft pillows don't amount to much and now he's left himself open for a straight shot to the kisser. Haley delivers, landing more knuckle than pillow this time and blood is drawn, and they're both grinning grotesquely—the cat watching from atop the dresser, the dog Bailey in the living room on the couch, avoiding confrontation as usual.

"Oh my god—sorry," says Haley as blood trickles out of Sam's mouth.

But she's not, really. Well, sorta, maybe. But kinda feels they may be even now, wondering if it was the $80 custom pillow by Tempur-Pedic that Monique had laid her slutty head on.

Noun & Verb

The noun is our friend. Take fork. Take pencil. Take duck. Dock. Pelican. Cake. Cat. Carpet. House. Wagon. Road. Adjectives are that gushing, well-meaning, but untrustworthy peer who says we were the best, most lyrical, most literate, mellifluous poet at the open mic last night, the absolute kindest person in the world, and the nicest friend ever…until we just don't know what to believe anymore. We know what we want to believe, sure. We also know we want another slice of cake, too, another tall glass of cold milk. But are we really hungry? Do adjectives and adverbs do anything else but make us want more? Add on a qualifying layer? Do they enhance, or make us wonder that whatever we thought was simply true, might just be otherwise? Sugary icing on sweet cake. Scaffolding on a building already painted. Check-on baggage when carry-on will do. The noun is our unadorned friend. The one we call in a pinch. The one who will tell us if our haircut sucks, if our complaining sounds like whining, if our brilliant stoner's-mind poem needs rewriting on a sober morning three days from now. Nouns show us the way. Verbs take us there, where the writing arrives at the end of the page, the pen having done its work, with dicey adjectives and just-in-case-you-didn't-get-it adverbs but mere tincture drops sparingly used. Unburdened by the gooey, by the gummy, by the show-off clatter of look-at-me similes, we return to the top of the page and read what before we only thought, but didn't know; what we felt but hadn't expressed; what we now clearly see and feel and trust and know. That's what friends are for. Verbs are the bees, nouns the flowers. A group of verbs is called a vibration, a group of nouns—a matter. Even a vibration needs to rest. Bees do sleep, by the way, and honey can stay true forever.

Pappy's Father's Day Carrot Cake

Pen-and-ink drawing by Tula Biederman

We've Got All Night

I'm cracking eggs and buttering bread and peeling tangerines, keeping an eye on the timer. Coffee cake is in the oven. The air smells cinnamon sweet, with a hint of something or other burning on the bottom of the stove, who knows. DJ is in her robe, out of bed for the first time all day, and so we're having breakfast for dinner. Her favorite meal. I'll be surprised if she eats more than a bite or two and doesn't just push the rest around the plate to make it look like her appetite has returned. It's dark outside. But not late according to the clock. These deep November nights feel late no matter the hour, the year still in descent. Dark and getting darker. Late and getting later. But I stop it right there. Not time, actually, but the thought descending. No need to go there. Negative will find you. So will grim. No need to stir that toxic stew. And then the timer beeps and this time I reach out and do stop time, for a moment, pulling out the coffee cake—DJ's recipe, the kitchen sweet with brown sugar cinnamon and DJ's smile. She inhales deeply, gratefully, and so do I. Time slows down. I set the cake on the counter to cool and admire the dark brown streaks on the golden surface. In no hurry. We've got all night.

Waiting for Results

Sitting in the sun on a patio made of stone, I open the dictionary and look up *benign*. It's already the most beautiful word in the English language. But with that silent *g*, that way of landing without ending, it sounds as if it alighted from another tongue, perhaps French, dropped in for a while, and stayed. Some words do that. The original name for Butterfly was Flutterby. Holding the dictionary in my lap, I sip green tea and watch a Monarch linger near the bottle brush tree. Butterflies have no mouths but taste through their feet. Some moths never eat, subsisting on stored energy from their youthful larvae days. These facts are new to me, the way the results of my labs will be. But whatever I have, I've had for a while. Today I'll just find out its name. Which makes today different from yesterday. That, and the way this butterfly now alights on my finger, wings gently pulsing, then flutters away.

The Lion Has Lost His Roar

He hops onto my lap after his morning meal, offering up a massive tabby head for petting, scratching, and stroking. He opens his jaw like he always has and mouths his formidable greatness, now with no sound…18 years…or 19, he's been through all the moves—the country house, the rented room, the floating home—orchards, solitary, & sea. He rises before dawn, eats in the dark, drinks and drinks, his ginger coat disheveled, his body growing thin, his roar gone silent. But as he sits across my lap and my work comes to a stop, in this moment, we all know who is king.

Little Bud, aka Cap'n Orange

Before There Were Poems

…there was an invisible web that stretched between us, long before the Internet, long before articulated words and Oxford commas and semicolon abuse and Hallmark, too. Before there were poems there were the shared looks, the contact without touching, the spark of understanding, the connection of mutual wisdom, the knowing, the mischievous grin, the shy look-away, the hand in the mouth—a single thumb, a finger, the whole drooly fist—and though we had no words to adorn our cries, our grunts, our laughter, those sounds were our language that delivered desire and carried the freight of feeling; but the eyes, the eyes said it all…before there were poems. *

** Class notes from a three-day seminar with Professor Penny, age four months*

Pierre's Step

Edible Grace

How do we know a fact is not also a fiction, a poem not also a prayer? I'm pushing a cart down the And/Or aisle of Stoner's Mind Department Store and discover just what I need—miscellaneous warnings and advice in bulk. I scoop them into a brown paper bag. Instantly they became a Quandary. My twin, who has come along, questions this, which is her right and which she always does, so we proceed to the front which could also be the back and ask the Fact Checker, who moonlights at Salvador Dali's Deli—famous for the world's tiniest sandwich so small it could fit in a matchbox, but so dense no one can lift it. So this leaves us with our Quandary, a collective noun undefined. An octopus, by the way, has three hearts and eight tentacles with minds of their own. Imagine the poetry an octopus could write, multiplied by eight. Imagine the pencils alone, ha! Our Fact Checker rings us up and asks if we want a receipt. We assure them we've had nothing to drink and we're pretty sure it's a fact. At the Care Facility, I visit a diminishing friend, and am mistaken for a patient. In a heartbeat, I sign out at the front desk and go for a bike ride in the breezy afternoon under a sky so blue just to prove I'm not. The jury's still out. So I write this poem and pray. My twin fits her shadow exactly into mine and for a moment we are one— with eight tentacles but only two hearts—and the need to dissect fact from fiction, poem from prayer means less than a tiny sandwich we can't eat. When in doubt we make cookie dough and lick the beaters. Is any art more beautiful than chocolate chip cookies baking in an oven, any truth greater than that sweet aroma filling the house? Edible grace, our ticket to the sun.

Elie Wiesel said writing is more like sculpture than painting—
you take away, you don't add. Living on houseboats
is the same. You take away what you don't need, leaving space
for beauty, wonder, and light to flow in, linger, and recede.

—Guy Biederman, in *This Day Afloat* (23 July 2017)

Publisher's Note: "Writing is for me not like painting; it's like sculpture…I carve away words until what is left is essential" by Elie Wiesel, as quoted in Rabbi Ariel Burger's journal/biography, *Witness: Lessons from Elie Wiesel's Classroom* (Houghton Mifflin Harcourt, 2018):

http://www.washingtonindependentreviewofbooks.com/index.php/features/witnessing-elie-wiesels-genius

End Notes

May 21, 2016: Farmer's Market Poet

At the small Friday Farmer's Market in nearby Mill Valley, a Greek woman sells produce from her family's farm in San Juan Bautista. I admire the Hearts of Romaine and she explains how she and her husband try to avoid bread and make their sandwiches with romaine, instead. Their 11-year-old son has decided he wants to eat his sandwiches that way, as well. And now his friends at school eat theirs that way, too. And I think, what wonderful parents and teachers. So natural. No insistence. The light falls on those who rise. Others notice, or don't. I look at the bin of summer squash, delicious looking and sweet. One is half yellow/half green. "Ah," she says, "that one was kissed by a zucchini!" She's a poet. I mention this. She says, "I never write anything down." And I think, not all poets are writers, & not all poems are written down.

—Guy Biederman, in *This Day Afloat*

About the Author

Guy Biederman teaches "low fat fiction" and is the author of three collections of short prose: *Soundings and Fathoms: Stories* (Finishing Line Press, 2018), *House Samurai* (Iota Press, 2006), and *Parts & Labor* (Thumbprint Press, 1992). His stories have appeared in dozens of venues including *Carve, daCunha, Flashback Fiction, KYSO Flash, Sea Letter, Third Wednesday,* and *Exposition Review,* where he was twice a Flash 405 winner. In 2018, his flash was nominated for the Best of the Net anthology.

Born in the Chihuahua desert near the Mexican border, Guy grew up on a stingray in Ventura, learned to write in the Peace Corps during a civil war in Guatemala, honed his craft pulling weeds and planting flowers as a gardener in San Francisco, and later received his M.A. from San Francisco State, where his teaching career began. He's been a creative-writing instructor since 1991, and he's also worked as a bookstore clerk, gardener, ad sales rep, sports writer, and publisher. For 12 years he published the literary magazine *Bust Out Stories* and a handful of books by Bay Area writers.

Guy hosts *The Floating Word* on Radio Sausalito, lives on a houseboat with his wife and two salty cats, and walks the planks daily.

Author's website: https://www.guybiederman.com/

His page at *daCunha*:
https://dacunha.global/author-guy-biederman/

See also his blog, *This Day Afloat: Reflections of Life on the Water*:
http://www.thisdayafloat.com/

Alpha List of Works

Credits

Page 21: "Tempur-Pedic" is a registered trademark belonging to Tempur-Pedic North America LLC.

"Bathrobe, Biscotti, & Bike" is reprinted from *Blue Fifth Review*, 2017 Fall Quarterly (17.12). "Pillow Fight" is reprinted from *Gathering Storm Magazine* (Issue 3, June 2017). "iPad Island," "Paper Clip Mechanics," and "Rue de la Bûcherie" are reprinted from *KYSO Flash* online (Issue 11, Spring 2019).

The following works are reprinted from Issue 12 of *KYSO Flash* online (Summer 2019): "Animal Ally," "Before There Were Poems," "Edible Grace," "How Do We Get Back Into the Zoo?" "Mr. Shortcut," "Noun & Verb," "The Lion Has Lost His Roar," "The Moose & the Fly," "Waiting for Results," "We've Got All Night," and "When You're Hungry Enough."

Pages 30 and 32: Excerpts are reprinted from Guy Biederman's blog, *This Day Afloat: Reflections of Life on the Water*.

Photographs:

Page 23: Pen-and-ink drawing, *Pappy's Father's Day Carrot Cake*, is copyrighted © 2015 Tula Biederman. All rights reserved. Reproduced within this book with permissions from both the artist and the author.

Images on the following pages are reproduced from *This Day Afloat* (with cropping by permission of the author/photographer):

- Covers: Houseboats (10 February 2016)
- Title Page: Whimsical breakfast, captioned "because I just can't help it sometimes" (1 October 2018)
- Page 18: *Breakfast at the Low Tide Café* (15 June 2018)
- Pages 26 and 27: *Little Bud, aka Cap'n Orange* (hanging out on the sofa with Bukowski's book *On Cats*; and patrolling the porch)
- Page 28: *Pierre's Step* (5 March 2017)
- Page 31: Knotholes (6 September 2017)

All web addresses in this book were tested and found valid
in August 2019, a few weeks before this book's release.

www.kysoflash.com

an online literary journal &

a micro-press of printed books

Knock-Your-Socks-Off Art and Literature